Holy in a Hurry

Holy in a Hurry

DAILY MEDITATIONS
ON THE PROPHECIES AND WISDOM
OF ST. JACINTA MARTO OF FATIMA

By Catherine Moran, OSF

BLUE ARMY PRESS

PUBLISHING DIVISION OF THE
WORLD APOSTOLATE OF FATIMA USA

ISBN: 979-8-9886377-7-6

The photo on the front cover of Jacinta Marto in 1917
is public domain.

Cover and text design by Sundae Graphic Design

Published in the United States by Blue Army Press.

World Apostolate of Fatima USA
P.O. Box 976, Washington, NJ 07882
www.bluearmy.com

Printed and bound in the United States of America

DEDICATION

To Dave, my beloved husband, soulmate and father of our five children, whose patience and love encouraged me to write this book. He would peek in the office and see me working at the computer or going through stacks of books and quietly close the door, leaving me to my research and writing.

ACKNOWLEDGEMENTS

First and foremost, I wish to thank St. Jacinta for her little inspirations when writing this book. I also want to thank my family and friends for advice and support. Finally, I want to thank my dear friend, Dorothy Carollo, who asked, 'Is it possible to write a meditation book on the recorded words of St. Jacinta?'

And I wish to acknowledge my dear friends Barb Ernster and Brenda Schwartz, who took time to read and help edit this book.

PREFACE

During her very short life, St. Jacinta rose to the heights of sanctity because of her complete acceptance of the Will of God in her life. God has given everyone a free will. The secret of attaining this high degree of sanctity is w=W, that is, our will equals God's Will. When we freely accept all that God sends and will send us with love, then we are on that road to sanctity. Like St. Jacinta, we are all called to be saints, but it is how we respond to that call that determines this. I like to think that St. Jacinta was holy in a hurry. At the age of 6 she had her first encounter with the mystical, and in four short years when she died, she became the youngest non-martyred saint in the history of the Church. Her life is an example for everyone. She has shown us that all that is required is for us to say 'yes' to God's Will in our lives, day by day, moment by moment, offering up everything for the salvation of poor sinners, especially those who have no one to pray for them.

The central theme of this little saint's holiness is a love of suffering. It is my prayer that through these meditations you learn to embrace her joy in suffering. This little saint offered all her sufferings as a means to save poor sinners. How did she do this? It was her burning love for the two Hearts of Jesus and Mary that enabled her to do this. She is our model and our help. When asked by Our Lady, "Are you willing to accept all that God will send you to save souls?" She answered enthusiastically, "Yes!" Her initial sufferings were voluntary; she would endure hunger and thirst to save souls. Later, her sufferings came from God by her illness. She gave us a powerful example of accepting suffering and crosses, when she was told by Our Lady she would die alone. She knew that was going to be a big sacrifice for her. In our most intense sufferings and fears, we need only reflect on St. Jacinta's fear of dying alone. We cannot comprehend how this thought terrified the young child. Many times, in tears she would sob at the thought of dying alone. It was Lucia who would remind her that this great offering would help save many souls. Lucia would say to her, "Don't you want to offer this up to the two Hearts to save souls?" Jacinta would immediately say "yes" and no longer complain. Many times, in our own pains and sorrows we falter and sometimes complain, "Why me Lord?" We need to stop and pray for strength to accept our crosses. St. Jacinta showed us it is 'ok' to sometimes fear our pains and sufferings, but like her we need to turn these fears over to the Immaculate Heart of Mary, who will then obtain for us the graces needed to offer this for the conversion of sinners.

Suffering is an integral part of our lives. Whether we want it or not, it is a part of the human condition. We suffer in our bodies, in our minds, in our hearts and in the very depths of souls. Our pains and sufferings come in many forms such as illness, fatigue, depression, anxiety, death of a loved one, betrayal, loneliness, failures in our undertakings, humiliations, spiritual dryness, and difficulty in our prayer life. All of these are a means to bring us closer to God and to save poor sinners. This 10-year-old little girl has shown us the way to embrace our own sufferings just as she did. We need to remember that St. Jacinta saw heaven when she saw Our Lady in 1917. She understood and did all that was required of her to reach heaven. We also have the words of St. Paul, who was taken to the third heaven, "Eye has not seen, ear has not heard, nor has it entered our hearts what God has prepared for those who love him!" (1 Cor 2:9). Think of these words the next time you are suffering and ask St. Jacinta to help you.

St. Jacinta has shown us by her examples why we should highly esteem all of our sufferings. For it is our sufferings offered with love that not only save our souls but help save the souls of poor sinners. In the gospels, Jesus said, "Blessed are they who suffer…" Think about it, without suffering, there is no virtue, no recompense, no salvation. Without suffering we can become attached to things of the world, forgetting our true home, heaven. This causes us to live only for the moment, ignoring eternity. Suffering endured patiently makes us holy and pleasing to God. For in our suffering, He sees His Divine Son in us. It is in our suffering that God consoles us. Finally, St. Jacinta, as with all the saints, shows us that suffering is the delight of the soul. Ask yourself, "How do I esteem suffering? How do I bear with what annoys me?" Resolve, like St. Jacinta, to cheerfully accept all the trials of your life.

The following meditations are quotes from St. Jacinta, as recorded by her cousin Ven. Sr. Lucia and Mother Maria da Purificação Godinho, who took care of St. Jacinta the last months of her life in Lisbon, Portugal. Mother Godinho, who was very much aware of the spiritual treasure she was graced to take care of, carefully recorded all that St. Jacinta said to her.

Fr. Andrew Apostoli, before he died, said this little saint saved thousands of souls from hell. Unfortunately, due to their many sins, the souls that were saved by her sacrifices and prayers are probably in purgatory. These souls must make reparation for their sins. God's justice demands it. The Church teaches that this is done either in this life or in purgatory. It is out of Christian charity and kindness that we pray for these poor souls suffering in purgatory. It is also a duty that we, the Church Militant, must pray for the Church Suffering so they may be released from their sufferings, thereby hastening their entrance into heaven

We are the only ones who can help these suffering, saved souls. We need to pray for them daily.

There are two themes in the many recorded words of St. Jacinta. First, a devotion and consecration to the Immaculate Heart of Mary. Second, a dedication to praying and suffering for poor souls who have no one to pray for them. You will read about these two important themes throughout this book of Meditations.

To summarize, in imitation of St. Jacinta, let us do the following:

1. Embrace her love, devotion and consecration to the Immaculate Heart of Mary.

2. Embody her love for praying and suffering to save poor souls from falling into hell, especially those souls who have no one to pray for them.

3. Continue to pray for the release of souls from purgatory, expediting their entrance into heaven.

We are truly blest to have her words of wisdom and prophecy to reflect and meditate upon. May these words and meditations help you grow in sanctity and holiness becoming like St. Jacinta, "Holy in a Hurry".

PRAYERS FOR DAILY USE

These prayers are suggested for your daily use. They were given at Fatima, or are related to helping you in your devotion to the Immaculate Heart of Mary.

The Morning Offering

O my God, in union with the Immaculate Heart of Mary (here kiss your Brown Scapular as a sign of your consecration – this carries a partial indulgence). I offer you the Precious Blood of Jesus from all the altars throughout the world, joining with it the offering of my every thought, word, and action of this day.

O my Jesus, I desire today to gain every indulgence and merit I can, and I offer them together with myself, to Mary Immaculate, that she may best apply them to the interests of Your Most Sacred Heart. Precious Blood of Jesus, save us! Sorrowful and Immaculate Heart of Mary, pray for us! Sacred Heart of Jesus, have mercy on us!

THE FATIMA PRAYERS

The Fatima Prayers were taught to the three children by the Angel of Peace in the spring and fall of 1916, and our heavenly Mother during the May – October apparitions. Sr. Lucia made them a part of her daily prayer life.

The Pardon Prayer

The angel taught this prayer in his first apparition.

My God, I believe, I adore, I hope, and I love Thee! I beg pardon for those who do not believe, do not adore, do not hope and do not love Thee. *(3 times)*

The Angel Prayer

The Angel taught this prayer, while bowing in adoration before a suspended Host and chalice.

O Most Holy Trinity, Father, Son and Holy Spirit, I adore Thee profoundly. I offer Thee the most precious Body, Blood, Soul and Divinity of Jesus Christ, present in all the tabernacles of the world, in reparation for the outrages, sacrileges and indifference by which He is offended. By the infinite merits of the Sacred Heart of Jesus and the Immaculate Heart of Mary, I beg the conversion of poor sinners.

The Eucharistic Prayer

On May 13, 1917, as Our Lady bathed the children in light, they were moved by an interior impulse to fall to their knees and say this prayer:

O Most Holy Trinity, I adore Thee! My God, my God, I love Thee in the most Blessed Sacrament!

Sacrifice Prayer

On June 13, 1917, Our Lady said to say this prayer whenever they made a sacrifice for Our Lord:

O Jesus, it is for love of Thee, for the conversion of sinners and in reparation for the sins committed against the Immaculate Heart of Mary.

Decade Prayer

On July 13, 1917, Our Lady taught the children to say this prayer after each decade of the Rosary:

O my Jesus, forgive us our sins, save us from the fires of hell. Lead all souls to heaven, especially those most in need of Thy mercy.

ADDITIONAL PRAYERS

Salvation Prayer
One of Jacinta's favorite and frequent prayers:

Sweet Heart of Mary, be my salvation. Immaculate Heart of Mary, convert sinners, save souls from hell.

Sr. Lucia's Prayer of Thanksgiving
My God, I love You in thanksgiving for the graces which You have granted me.

Sister Lucia's Prayer to the Immaculate Heart
Your Immaculate Heart, O Mother of all tenderness, and next to your altar I will always invoke your protection, your name, Mary, your sweet Heart.

Novena to Our Lady of Fatima
From the 4th – 12th day of every month, Sr. Lucia would begin a special novena to Our Lady of Fatima in anticipation of the 13th day: One Memorare and three Hail Marys in honor of the Holy Trinity.

Memorare
Remember, O most gracious Virgin Mary, that never was it known that anyone who fled to your protection, implored your help, or sought your intercession was left unaided. Inspired by this confidence, I fly unto you, O Virgin of virgins, my mother; to you do I come, before you I stand, sinful and sorrowful. O Mother of the Word Incarnate, despise not my petitions, but in your mercy hear and answer me.

Consecration to the Immaculate Heart of Mary by Ven. Pope Pius XII

Most Holy Virgin Mary, tender Mother of men, to fulfill the desires of the Sacred Heart of Jesus and the request of the Vicar of Your Son on earth, we consecrate ourselves and our families to your Sorrowful and Immaculate Heart, O Queen of the Most Holy Rosary, and we recommend to You all the people of our country and all the world.

Please accept our consecration, dearest Mother, and use us as you wish to accomplish Your designs in the world.

O Sorrowful and Immaculate Heart of Mary, Queen of the Most Holy Rosary, and Queen of the World, rule over us, together with the Sacred Heart of Jesus Christ, Our King. Save us from the spreading flood of modern paganism; kindle in our hearts and homes the love of purity, the practice of a virtuous life, an ardent zeal for souls, and a desire to pray the Rosary more faithfully.

We come with confidence to You, O Throne of Grace and Mother of Fair Love. Inflame us with the same Divine Fire which has inflamed your own Sorrowful and Immaculate Heart. Make our hearts and homes your shrine, and through us, make the Heart of Jesus, together with your rule, triumph in every heart and home. Amen.

FIRST SATURDAY DEVOTION

On December 10, 1925, at the Dorothean convent in Pontevedra, Spain, Our Lady appeared to Sr. Lucia, fulfilling her promise from July 13, 1917 that she would return to ask for the Communions of Reparation on first Saturdays.

She appeared with the Child Jesus standing at her side, enthroned in a cloud of light. The Mother of God showed Lucia her Heart encircled by thorns and the Child Jesus said, "Have compassion on the Heart of your most holy Mother covered with thorns, with which ungrateful men pierce it at every moment, and there is no one to make an act of reparation to remove them."

Then Our Lady held out her Heart and said, "Look, my daughter, at my Heart, surrounded with thorns with which ungrateful men pierce me at every moment by their blasphemies and ingratitude. You at least try to console me and say that I promise to assist at the hour of death, with the graces necessary for salvation, all those who, on the first Saturday of five consecutive months, shall confess, receive Holy Communion, recite five decades of the Rosary and keep me company for fifteen minutes while meditating on the mysteries of the Rosary, with the intention of making reparation to me."

Lucia was asked by her confessor, why Our Lady requested five First Saturdays? During the night of May 29, 1930, Sr. Lucia was in the chapel praying about this. She wrote, "I felt myself being more possessed by the Divine Presence, and if I am not mistaken, the following was revealed to me:

'My daughter, the motive is simple: there are five ways in which people offend and blaspheme against the Immaculate Heart of Mary:

1. Blasphemies against the Immaculate Conception,
2. Blasphemies against her Perpetual Virginity,
3. Blasphemies against her Divine Maternity, refusing at the same to accept her as the Mother of all mankind,
4. Those who try publicly to implant in the heart of children indifference, contempt and even hate against this Immaculate Mother,
5. Those who insult her directly in her sacred images.

Here, my daughter, is the motive why the Immaculate Heart of Mary asked me for this act of reparation and to move my mercy to forgive those souls who had the misfortune of offending her. As for you, try incessantly with all your prayers and sacrifices to move me into mercifulness toward those poor souls.'

It is important for everyone to make the five First Saturdays of reparation to obtain Our Lady's "Great Promise" of providing graces at the time of death. Then, continue to do the First Saturdays, especially to obtain graces for the conversion and salvation of other souls. Its regular practice places you in a habit of monthly confession and helps you form an intimate and personal relationship with the Immaculate Heart of Mary, a sign of your devotion to her.

DAILY MEDITATIONS

The daily quotations on the wisdom and prophecy of St. Jacinta are from Ven. Sr. Lucia's writings and the writings of Mother Maria da Purificação Godinho, director of the orphanage (convent) connected to the Church of Our Lady of the Miracles. She was a Franciscan nun who wore civilian clothes and had to change the word "convent" to "orphanage" because of the government restrictions on religious. She later became a Poor Claire nun and died on June 6, 1960.

The meditation following each quote is to help draw you further into reflection on what St. Jacinta is trying to teach you. Allow the Holy Spirit to further guide and enlighten you. The meditations are the fruits of Eucharistic adoration. I encourage all who read this book to spend time in adoration. Many graces and blessings are given to those who visit and adore Our Lord in this Blessed Sacrament of His love.

After each meditation there is a Daily Challenge, which helps you put into practice the theme of the meditation throughout your day. The Daily Challenge leads you into a deeper commitment in your prayer life. In turn, this draws you closer to the love of the Sacred Hearts of Jesus and Mary. As part of your challenge to grow, incorporate the prayers and devotions in the Appendix as a part of your regular prayer life.

Throughout the day, ask Our Lady to help you to grow in virtue and in the love of God. With her help, you can walk the path of love and sacrifice that will lead you ultimately to your eternal home—heaven.

1. When asked why she liked being among the sheep, St. Jacinta said, *"I want to do the same as Our Lord in the holy picture they gave me. He's just like this in the middle of them all and He's holding one of them in His arms."*

MEDITATION

St. Jacinta loved to hold tightly the little white lambs, kissing them. At night on their way home, she would carry them on her shoulders so they would not get tired. She did this in imitation of Our Lord in the holy picture that was given to her. In Luke 15:2-7, Our Lord told them this parable: "Which one of you, having a hundred sheep and losing one of them, does not leave the ninety-nine in the wilderness and go after the one that is lost until he finds it? When he has found it, he lays it on his shoulders and rejoices. And when he comes home, he calls together his friends and neighbors, saying to them, 'Rejoice with me, for I have found my sheep that was lost.'" How wonderful the world would be today if everyone strived to imitate Our Lord in all their thoughts, words and actions. We have His words in Sacred Scripture on how we are to live: "Take my yoke upon you and learn from me for I am meek and humble of heart and you will find rest for your souls." (Mt 11:29)

DAILY CHALLENGE

Today before doing anything, first ask yourself, "What would Jesus do?"

2. Lucia after having been to mass, was walking past
Jacinta's house, Jacinta said to her,
*"Come over here close to me, for you have the
hidden Jesus in your heart."*

MEDITATION

St. Jacinta's first Holy Communion was from the Angel of Fatima in the fall of 1916. She was 6 years old. After the apparitions, she received the Sacrament of First Holy Communion in the Church in 1918 and was able to receive Communion several times before her death. Our Lady revealed to St. Jacinta knew the day and time she would die, yet she was denied Holy Communion on the night of her death. The priest, thinking she would not die that night, told her he would bring the Eucharist to her the next day. Meditate on that fact that Jacinta never committed a mortal sin. She preserved her baptismal innocence to her death. Our Lord never left that beautiful, pure soul. How often do you reflect on your First Communion and what it meant to you? Like St. Jacinta, do you hunger for the Hidden Jesus?

DAILY CHALLENGE

Resolve today to receive Communion often, so you too can have the hidden Jesus in your heart.

3. St. Jacinta said to her cousin and brother,
"Have you been forgetting to tell Our Lord how much you love Him for the graces He has given us?"

MEDITATION

These words of St. Jacinta echo down to the present time. St. Paul in his letter to the Ephesians (4:7), wrote: "Grace is given to each person according to the measure of Christ's gift." St. John Fisher told us where grace comes from: "Grace is favor, the free and undeserved help that God gives us to respond to His call to become children of God, adoptive sons, partakers of the divine nature and of eternal life." St. Augustine captured this yearning for God's grace when he wrote: "Lord, you have made us for yourself, and our hearts are restless until they find their rest in you." How rarely do people of the world think of Our Lord, much less thank Him for the many blessings He gives them every day. How often do you thank Our Lord for the many graces He has given you? We are all called to live in the presence of God. These words of St. Jacinta gently remind us of how to do this.

DAILY CHALLENGE

Try often during the day to take a moment and tell Jesus how much you love Him for all the graces He has given you, especially at the very moment a grace is given to you.

4. *"So many people falling into hell!*
So many people in hell."

MEDITATION

These are the words of St. Jacinta after she experienced the vision of hell, which forever changed her short life. In the gospels, Our Lord mentions hell fifteen times and referred to it with words such as flame, fire, destruction and condemnation. Yet people today do not believe in the existence of hell, or the eternity of hell. This truly is the Satan's greatest hoax, 'There is no hell.' Our Lord told St. Faustina, "The loss of each soul plunges me into mortal sadness." St. Faustina added to this; "O my God, how I pity those people who do not believe in eternal life."

DAILY CHALLENGE:

We all know someone who does not believe in the existence of hell and are in great need of God's mercy. Pray for this person today.

5. *"Poor Holy Father, we must pray very much for him."*

MEDITATION

The pope is the visible head of the Church, the Mystical Body of Christ. In the third secret, the three children saw a man dressed in white being persecuted and killed. They understood this man was the pope. Pope St. John Paul II, after the attempt on his life, realized that he was the pope in the vision and it was the hand of the Immaculate Heart of Mary that saved his life on May 13, 1981, from an assassin's bullet. It was also through the prayers of everyone who prays for the pope that his life was preserved, enabling him to narrowly escape death that day. He went on to read and promote the Fatima message for the rest of his life.

DAILY CHALLENGE

The Holy Father still needs our daily prayers and sacrifices. Today try to remember to say a prayer for the pope, Christ's vicar on earth.

6. *"Tell everyone that God grants us graces through the Immaculate Heart of Mary; that people are to ask her for them; and that the heart of Jesus wants the Immaculate Heart of Mary to be venerated at His side."*

MEDITATION

Notice that St. Jacinta said, "The heart of Jesus wants the Immaculate Heart of Mary to be venerated at His side." He wishes us to *venerate*, not *worship* the Immaculate Heart of Mary. To venerate means to give honor and to regard with great respect. To worship means to adore and glorify God alone. We do not worship any other being but the Holy Trinity. We venerate the Blessed Virgin Mary and the saints. Jesus has stated that He wishes His Mother's Immaculate Heart is to be venerated together with His Sacred Heart. According to St. John Eudes, these two hearts are inseparable. This saint often referred to these two Hearts as one Heart.

DAILY CHALLENGE

Think often today of the love that the two Hearts of Jesus and Mary have for you. What small sacrifice can you do today to console these two Hearts?

7. *"Tell them also to pray to the Immaculate Heart of Mary for peace since God has entrusted it to her."*

MEDITATION

This concept is further explained to us by St. Louis de Montfort when he wrote: *"But Mary's power over the evil spirits will especially shine forth in the latter times, when Satan will lie in wait for her heel, that is for her humble servants and her poor children whom she will rouse to fight against him. They will be rich in God's graces, which will be abundantly bestowed on them by Mary. They will be great and exalted before God in holiness. They will be superior to all creatures by their great zeal and so strongly will they be imparted by divine assistance that in union with Mary, they will crush the head of Satan with their heel, that is their humility, and bring victory to Jesus Christ."* Bringing about peace and the Triumph of the Immaculate Heart of Mary is so simple. She gave us her peace plan from heaven in 1917: pray the rosary every day, wear your brown scapular, do your daily duty, and do the five First Saturdays of Reparation, at least once.

DAILY CHALLENGE

Are you committed to doing what Our Lady asked of you at Fatima? Begin today by doing what she has asked of everyone to obtain peace in the world.

8. *"Oh if I could only put into everybody's heart the burning fire I have inside me which makes me love the Hearts of Jesus and Mary so much."*

MEDITATION

Of this burning fire, St. Gemma Galgoni wrote: "It is, however, a fire that does not torment me, rather it delights me." Concerning this burning fire, Our Lord told St. Margaret Mary while praying before the Blessed Sacrament: "My Divine Heart is so inflamed with love for men and for you in particular that, being unable any longer to contain within itself the flames of its burning charity, it must spread them abroad by your means, and manifest itself to [mankind] in order to enrich them with the precious graces of sanctification and salvation...." It is this burning love that St. Jacinta wishes to give all of us. We are all called to this all- consuming fire of Divine Love, but God is waiting for you to freely accept this great gift.

DAILY CHALLENGE

If you are fighting silent battles in your life today, try to remember to try to see all your crosses and sufferings coming from the hand of God who ordains and permits these from motives and love for you. Ask yourself, 'What prayers and sacrifices will I accept today to help me grow in my love for God?'

9. *"Hell, hell. How sorry I am for the souls that are going to hell. The souls burn there alive like wood on a fire."*

MEDITATION

St. Faustina saw hell and described it in her diary: "The kinds of tortures I saw: the first torture that constitutes hell is the loss of God; the second is perpetual remorse of conscience; the third is that one's condition will never change; the fourth is the fire that will penetrate the soul without destroying it, a terrible suffering, since it is a purely spiritual fire lit by God's anger; the fifth torture is conditional darkness and a terrible suffocating smell, and despite the darkness, the devils and the souls of the damned see each other and all the evil, both of others and their own; the sixth torture is the constant company of Satan, the seventh torture is horrible despair, hatred of God, vile words, curses and blasphemies. These are the tortures suffered by all the damned together."

DAILY CHALLENGE

In imitation of St. Jacinta pray with confidence and mercy the prayer taught to her by Our Lady: "O my Jesus forgive us our sins, save us from the fires of hell, lead all souls to heaven, especially those in most need of your mercy."

10. *"Of the war that is coming, of the many people who are going to die and go to hell. What a shame! If they would stop offending God neither the war would come, nor would they go to hell."*

MEDITATION

It has been said, "War is hell." Jacinta knew that both war and hell came from the disorder of sin. St. Paul in his letter to the Romans (6:23) wrote, "For the wages of sin is death." The 20th century was a time of wars and death beyond all human understanding. That century witnessed man's inhumanity to mankind. Our Lord said, "For nothing is hidden that will not be made manifest, nor is anything secret that will not be known and come to light." (Lk 8:17) The means to prevent this was to turn to the Immaculate Heart of Mary, the complete opposite of war and hell. The world today is still in a constant state of war, which is hell on earth. To change this, we need generous souls to offer sacrifice and prayer for the conversion of sinners.

DAILY CHALLENGE

All sin has an effect on the whole world, even private sin. All our actions have real consequences. In imitation of St. Jacinta what can you do today to counter the consequences of sin and bring about this conversion to save souls?

11. On suffering: *"Our Lady wants me to go to two hospitals. But it is not to be cured. It is to suffer more for the love of Our Lord and for sinners."*

MEDITATION

St. Jacinta understood that God permits us to suffer to obtain the virtue of humility and make us more Christ-like. She also realized that so many people have turned away from the love of Jesus and all He has done for our salvation. St. John Vianney wrote, "Nothing afflicts the heart of Jesus so much as to see all His sufferings of no avail to so many." We can wonder how this little girl could not only suffer patiently but ask for and embrace this great suffering. St. Gemma Galgoni answered this for us when she said, "If you really want to love Jesus, first learn to suffer, because suffering teaches you to love." This is the answer for St. Jacinta's great love of suffering.

DAILY CHALLENGE

Understanding and enduring all the suffering sent to you by God requires a peaceful and serene soul. Today, try to look at insults and suffering as an opportunity to practice the art of serenity and acceptance.

12. On fear: *"I shall go to Lisbon, to another hospital. I won't see you or my parents again. When I suffer a great deal, I shall be alone, but I must not be afraid, because she will come to take me to heaven. I shall never see you again. You won't see me. Oh, pray for me for I shall die alone…"*

MEDITATION

Concerning this sacrifice of dying alone, St. Jacinta cried out, "Oh Jesus now you can convert many sinners because this great sacrifice is such a big one." What is your greatest fear? Do you run from it, or do you embrace it like St. Jacinta did? She did not allow this fear to overwhelm her but trusted in the love and protection of the Immaculate Heart of Mary. She looked beyond her fear to the souls she would help save from the fires of hell. The words, "Be not afraid" are in Scripture 366 times. Remember that all your sacrifices and acts of love, no matter how small, matter to God. Your fear is nothing but a lack of trust in God and in His loving Divine Providence.

DAILY CHALLENGE

Reflect today on the words of St. Teresa of Avila, "Let nothing perturb you, let nothing frighten you. All things pass. God does not change. Patience achieves everything."

13. Appreciating the Eucharist:
"Am I going to die without receiving the hidden Jesus?
If only Our Lady would bring Him to me, when she comes
to take me to heaven."

MEDITATION

The noted 19th century Anglican convert, Father Frederick William Faber, wrote, "One Holy Communion is enough to make a saint." St. Imelda Lambertini, patroness of first communicants, died in ecstasy after receiving her first Communion. She was 11-years-old. St. Jacinta received her first Communion from the Angel of Peace in 1916. Yet her desire to receive Communion consumed her until the day she died. This is why Jacinta is a saint. St. Ignatius of Loyola wrote, "One of the most admirable effects of Holy Communion is to preserve the soul from sin, and to help those who fall through weakness to rise again." What is keeping you from receiving Communion often if not every day? Every day we are given the opportunity to receive Our Lord in Holy Communion at daily Mass. Think often on the words of St. Maximilian Kolbe, "If angels could be jealous of men, they would be so for one reason: Holy Communion."

DAILY CHALLENGE

Today make your angel "jealous" by receiving Holy Communion.

14. *"Our poor dear Lord! I'll never sin again!*
I don't want Our Lord to suffer any more."

MEDITATION

With tears in her eyes, this is what St. Jacinta exclaimed after Lucia told her about the sufferings of Our Lord. St. Jacinta is not the only saint to shed tears over sins. We have St. Mary Magdalene weeping at the feet of Jesus, St. Peter weeping bitterly after denying Our Lord, and King David over his sin with Bathsheba. Countless saints have cried because of their sins and the pain it caused Jesus during His passion and death. How often do you think about your own sins, and the pain and suffering it caused our dear Lord? The Church in her infinite wisdom has set aside the 40 days of Lent for this purpose. You should often, especially on Fridays, meditate and console Our Savior for the sufferings He endured for our salvation.

DAILY CHALLENGE

Today in imitation of St. Jacinta, resolve to have a deep regret for having offended God, and make a firm commitment to not sin again. If possible, go to confession.

15. *"Wars are only punishments for the sins of the world,"* St. Jacinta said one time. *"Our Lady cannot stay the arm of her beloved Son upon the world anymore. It is necessary to do penance. If the people amend themselves, our Lord shall still come to the aid of the world. If they do not amend themselves, punishment shall come."*

MEDITATION

Again one is struck by the similarity between Jacinta's words and the words of Our Lady of La Salette, "If my people will not submit, I shall be forced to let go the hand of my Son." Our Lady continued: "How long have I suffered for you! If my Son is not to abandon you, I am obliged to entreat him without ceasing. But you take no heed of that. No matter how well you pray in the future, no matter how well you act, you will never be able to make up what I have endured on your behalf." These words of Our Lady have echoed down to Fatima in 1917 and in the third secret of Fatima. The Triumph of her Immaculate Heart will come about along with an era of peace, but only when enough people do as she has asked.

DAILY CHALLENGE

The road to sanctity can be very difficult and when you are having a rough day, think of your Heavenly Mother – shedding tears for you! Reflect on how she prays and intercedes unceasingly for you, her beloved child. Today make an effort to do as she has requested to bring about the triumph of her Immaculate Heart.

16. When St. Jacinta asked about the sins that send
a soul to hell, Lucia told her, *"Perhaps not going to
mass on Sundays; stealing, saying wicked words, cursing,
swearing."* Jacinta responded, *"And for only one word
they can go to hell? What would it cost them to keep quiet
and go to mass? I am sorry for sinners. Oh, if I could only
let them see hell."*

MEDITATION

In her apparition in 1840, one of the complaints of Our Lady of La Salette was the total disregard of keeping Holy the Sabbath. *"I have given you six days to work. The seventh I have reserved for myself, yet no one will give it to me. This is what causes the weight of my Son's arm to be so heavy."* One of the main reasons souls are falling into hell was given to us by St. Padre Pio. Asked what he thought of people who did not believe in hell, he wisely replied: *"They will very well believe in hell when they get there."* To this statement, St. Faustina added: *"But I noticed one thing: that most of the souls there are those who disbelieved that there is a hell."*

DAILY CHALLENGE

This is something very important to meditate upon: that it only takes one unrepented mortal sin to send a soul to hell for all eternity. As you go about your day today, pause often and say one *Hail Mary* for a soul in danger of going to hell at that moment.

17. When she heard people cursing, she would cry out, *"O my God, don't the people realize this kind of talk might send them to hell? Forgive them Jesus and convert them. They certainly don't know they are offending you."*

MEDITATION

In 1840, Our Lady of La Salette tearfully complained to the two children, Melanie and Maximum: *"The cart drivers cannot swear without bringing in my Son's name. These are the two things that make my Son's arm so heavy."* Unfortunately, today cursing and swearing are an everyday occurrence. It is on TV, the movies, social media and in society in general. St. Paul warns us: "But now put them all away: anger, wrath, malice, slander, and foul talk from your mouth." (Col. 3:8) And in Ephesians, "Let no evil talk come out of your mouths, but only such as is good for edifying, as fits the occasion, that it may impart grace to those who hear." (Eph 4:29) St. Jacinta was very much aware of hell as representing God's justice and the Immaculate Heart of Mary representing His mercy.

DAILY CHALLENGE

It is not commonly known, but St. Joan of Arc is the Patron Saint of Profanity, probably because of the profanity she heard coming from the mouths of the French soldiers. Pray to her for those you hear cursing, swearing, and taking the name of God in vain. When you hear someone taking God's name in vain, pray quietly in reparation: *"Admirably and holy is the name of God."*

18. When St. Jacinta was sick and was encouraged to eat, she said, *"No, I am offering this sacrifice for those who eat too much."*

MEDITATION

The sin of gluttony is one of the seven capital sins. It is an inordinate love of eating and drinking. Our Savior warns us against this vice, saying, "Take heed to yourselves lest your hearts be overcharged with surfeiting and drunkenness, and the cares of this life." (Lk. 21:34) When you are fasting, think of the gall and vinegar which were given to Our Savior on the cross to drink. Reflect on the fact that Our Lord fasted 40 days and 40 nights in the desert before beginning His public life. The saints understood the spiritual value in fasting. St. Ambrose said, "Fasting is the death of sin, the destruction of our crimes, and the remedy of our salvation." While St. Jerome remarked, "Fasting and sackcloth are the arms of penance, the help of sinners." Finally, St. Augustine wrote, "No one fasts for human praise, but for the pardon of his sins."

DAILY CHALLENGE

Today, try fasting from little things. For example, skip dessert, eat what is given to you, even if you do not care for it, and do not eat until you are full. You can also fast by refraining from saying unkind words and keeping your opinion to yourself.

19. St. Jacinta, on seeing the pain she caused Lucia when she told her family about seeing the "lady" on May 13, tearfully exclaimed, *"I did wrong, I won't say anymore to anybody."*

MEDITATION

Lucia, writing on this incident in her memoirs, said that Jacinta knelt down in front of her and crying, lifted up her hands to beg pardon for the pain she had caused her cousin. This was a great act of humility on Jacinta's part. After this incident, she never again spoke of the visions to anyone. On the importance of the virtue of humility, St. Augustine wrote, "It was pride that changed angels into devils; it is humility that makes men as angels." How often do we cause others pain and never think about it, much less apologize asking for forgiveness?

DAILY CHALLENGE

Who have you offended by your callous and indifferent remarks? Today pray for those you have hurt by your sins. If possible, apologize and ask for their forgiveness.

20. St. Jacinta during her surgery under a local anesthetic – *"Oh my Jesus! Oh my God!"*

MEDITATION

Many times when one is in great pain, they either curse and swear or cry out to God for His help. St. Ignatius Loyola wrote, "If God sends you many sufferings, it is a sign that He has great plans for you and certainly wants to make you a saint." This truly applied to St. Jacinta. It was through her intense sufferings that she saved souls and climbed the heights of sanctity. But this applies to all of us. St. Sebastian Valfre said, "When it is all over you will not regret having suffered; rather you will regret having suffered so little, and suffered that little so badly." St. Faustina tells us that the greater the suffering, the purer the love. This truly was the case with St. Jacinta, whose pure love helped to save souls.

DAILY CHALLENGE

St. Gemma Galgoni said, "If you really want to love Jesus, first learn to suffer, because suffering teaches you to love." What can you accept today to increase your love for Jesus?

21. On heaven: *"Yes, I know I am going to heaven,*
but I also want everyone to go there."

MEDITATION

St. Jacinta's knowledge that she was going to heaven was a great gift of grace from Our Lady. Seeing Our Lady was like being in heaven for the three children. Little Jacinta wanted to share this joy with everyone. She truly understood the words of St. Paul, "Eye has not seen, nor has ear heard, nor has it entered into the heart of man what God has prepared for those who love him." (1 Cor 2:9) But St. Thomas More gave us more insight into heaven when he wrote: "Earth hath no sorrow that heaven cannot heal." Like St. Jacinta, we all need to keep our eyes on our true home, heaven.

DAILY CHALLENGE

How often do you think of heaven? Today, remind yourself that you are only a traveler here on earth and that heaven is your true home.

22. *"Many marriages are not good; they do not please our Lord and are not of God."*

MEDITATION

Today we are witnessing the Seventh Commandment, thou shalt not commit adultery, held up to ridicule in the media, movies, TV, books, social media and the internet. Today one marriage in three ends in a divorce, which is a flagrant disregard of God's laws. It is common today to hear people say this is my second, third, or fourth marriage. In John's gospel, Our Lord told the woman at the well, "Go, call your husband and come back." "I have no husband," she replied. Jesus said to her, "You are right when you say you have no husband. The fact is, you have had five husbands, and the man you now have is not your husband." (Jn 4: 17-18) On October 13, 1951, Ven. Pope Pius XII gave us the solution to this problem. Over the radio to the pilgrims at Fatima he said: "The Virgin Mother's insistence on the recitation of the family rosary was meant to teach us that the secret of peace in family life lies in imitating the virtues of the Holy Family."

DAILY CHALLENGE

Ven. Sr. Lucia, before she died, told us that Satan's final assault would be against marriage and the family. Today, try to pray for those who respond to the call of the vocation of marriage, for good marriages, and especially pray for those who are married and are struggling in their marriage vocation.

23. Kissing her crucifix, Jacinta would exclaim:
*"Oh Jesus, I love you and I want to suffer a great deal
for love of you."*

MEDITATION

Many saints during times of great suffering would embrace and kiss the crucifix. They all had one goal – to suffer for the love of Christ crucified. St. Jacinta was no different in the way she embraced her sufferings. We, though, cannot understand the sufferings of the saints because of our own limited capacity to bear pain and suffering. We have yet to reach their level of love and sacrifice. The old saying, 'the spirit is willing but the flesh is weak,' applies to all of us. We are all weighed down by our own timidity and the luxuries of the modern world. We shrink from suffering, yet we only have to look to Jesus on the cross for the graces we need to accept all the sufferings sent to us. Hardships, terrors and all forms of suffering melt away before a firm, resolute and brave character.

DAILY CHALLENGE

Today, try to embrace your daily cross by first looking at the crucifix and asking for the grace to love and embrace that cross.

24. Every day the nurses had to tend to Jacinta's gaping wound, on her side which caused her excruciating pain. As they were taking care of her, in pain Jacinta groaned softly, *"O my good mother, oh my good mother. Patience, we must all suffer to go to heaven."*

MEDITATION

St. Albert the Great wrote, "True and perfect patience consists in the readiness to sustain difficulties, hardship, and injustices; not only when one deserves them, but even when they are completely underserved." This virtue, which St. Paul lists as one of the fruits of the Spirit, is necessary and goes hand in hand with suffering. It was St. Therese, the little flower, who said, "I do not know how we get to heaven without suffering." This was the belief of all the saints. The great St. Teresa of Avila also tells us, "Suffering is a great favor. Remember that everything soon comes to an end ... and take courage. Think of how our gain is eternal." This is what St. Jacinta is telling all of us. Suffering patiently, with love, is the road to heaven.

DAILY CHALLENGE

Remember that what you do with the sufferings and trials that will come your way today will determine your eternal happiness in heaven.

25. *"Certain fashions are going to be introduced which will offend Our Lord very much. Those who serve God should not follow these fashions. The Church has no fashions; Our Lord is always the same."*

MEDITATION

Jacinta's warning here, was not referring to how we dress, but was referring to the many fashions of the world that offend God. Today, we have many 'fashions' that offend God. For example: materialism, secularism, relativism, humanism, racism, and atheism. To that, can be added, obsessions with wealth, money, power, youthfulness, immorality and hedonistic lifestyles of the world today. St. John the Evangelist warned us, "Do not love things of the world...for the world and its enticements are passing away." St. Ignatius of Antioch understood this when he wrote, "No earthly pleasures, no kingdoms of this world can benefit me in any way." Our example of living the Fatima message is what the world needs to see today.

DAILY CHALLENGE

Today, challenge yourself to live and practice your faith, even when it is difficult.

26. St. Jacinta said to Lucia one day,
*"Don't you see many, many roads, highways and fields
jammed with people weeping with hunger for they have
nothing to eat? And the Holy Father praying in a church
before the Immaculate Heart of Mary? And many people
praying with him?"*

MEDITATION

This particular vision of St. Jacinta contains much fruit to meditate upon. The hunger she was referring to in this vision was spiritual hunger. In the Beatitudes, Jesus said, "Blessed are those who hunger and thirst for righteousness, for they shall be satisfied." St. Paul advised the Ephesians to satisfy their spiritual hunger by turning away from evil and living lives of love, kindness, compassion, and forgiveness. We need to keep our focus on Jesus in the Blessed Sacrament, with frequent reception of Holy Communion and a daily prayer life to sustain our spiritual life.

DAILY CHALLENGE

Today, and every day, you should be asking yourself, 'What am I doing to keep myself spiritually strong and close to God?'

27. *"If I could only put into the hearts of all the fire that is burning within my own heart, and that makes me love the Hearts of Jesus and Mary so very much!"*

MEDITATION

Sadly, so few souls burn with this fire of love for the Hearts of Jesus and Mary. Yet, many saints experienced this mystical phenomenon described by St. Jacinta. Like her, at times, their love for God was so vehement that their heart would burn with divine love. St. Gemma Galgoni described this divine fire of love as "a fire that does not torment me, rather it delights me, but it also exhausts and consumes me." This is why St. Jacinta desired to put into all hearts this fire of Divine Love, so that everyone would be consumed with the love of the Hearts of Jesus and Mary.

DAILY CHALLENGE

Today, pray and ask for the fire of Divine Love for the Hearts of Jesus and Mary to come into your own heart.

28. Despite St. Jacinta's illness, she often made
painful trips to the Cova and also to Mass.
"Don't try to come to Mass," Lucia said one day,
"it's too much for you. Besides, it isn't Sunday."
Jacinta replied, *"That doesn't matter. I want to go in
place of the sinners who don't go even on Sundays."*

MEDITATION

These words coming from the lips of this favored child of Mary
remind us that the desecration of the Sabbath was one of the
sins against which Our Lady had protested at La Salette. Our
Lady wept profusely throughout the apparition, one of the few
apparitions in which she cried. St. Jacinta was painfully aware
of the disregard of people keeping Sundays holy by attending
Mass. St. Padre Pio said, "The world could more easily exist
without the sun than without the Mass." St. John Vianney, the
patron of parish priests, proclaimed, "If we knew the value of
the Holy Mass, what a great effort we would make to attend it!"

DAILY CHALLENGE

Do you only go to Mass on Sunday, or do you try to go during
the week if possible? One of the saints wrote that all our masses
will go before us when we die, pleading our cause before God.
We all need to ask ourselves, "How much do I value the Mass?"

29. "Tell everyone that Our Lord grants us all graces through the Immaculate Heart of Mary, that we are to ask her for them."

MEDITATION

One of the most beautiful aspects of the Fatima message is the devotion to the Immaculate Heart of Mary. It is through His mother's most tender and loving heart that all graces are given to us. St. Jacinta was so ravished by the goodness and the love of the Immaculate Heart of our heavenly Mother, she would cry out, "I love the Immaculate Heart of Mary!" This is the essence and the secret of her rapid progress in holiness and sanctity. Whatever you need, whether physical, emotional or spiritual, do as St. Jacinta; go to this loving Mother's heart and ask, and you shall receive.

DAILY CHALLENGE

What do you need to do in your life today to bring you closer to the love of the Hearts of Jesus and Mary? Go to a quiet place, close your eyes and ask.

30. *"I don't know how it is that I feel Our Lord inside of me. I understand what He tells me, but I do not see or hear Him. But it is so good to be with Him."*

MEDITATION

Like St. Jacinta, we all have Jesus within us, but it is what we do and how we respond to His presence within us that defines who we are. We experience the presence of God in special ways. Sometimes, we experience feelings of peace and joy that are beyond words. We can experience the presence of God through a song or through scripture. When this happens, it is the Holy Spirit who brings this grace to us. This is called the manifest presence of God because He is with us in a clear and convincing way. Embrace this gift when it happens and like St. Jacinta say, "It is so good to be with Him."

DAILY CHALLENGE

Today, reflect and meditate on God's presence within you using the following from St. Paul's letter to the Corinthians: "For we are the temple of the living God; as God said, 'I will make my dwelling among them and walk among them, and I will be their God, and they shall be my people.'" (2 Cor 6:15)

31. Jacinta told Lucia: *"Soon I shall go to heaven. You are to stay here to reveal that the Lord wants to establish the devotion to the Immaculate Heart of Mary...Tell them to ask for peace from the Immaculate Heart of Mary, as God has entrusted it to her."*

MEDITATION

An important aspect of the Fatima message is the promise of peace for the world through the Immaculate Heart of Mary. This is God's Will and desire. How is this to come about? The answer was given to Ven. Sr. Lucia by Jesus on December 10, 1925 – the request for the Five First Saturdays of Reparation to the Heart of Mary. Before Sr. Lucia died, she said not enough people are doing the Five First Saturdays and that is why we have not seen the triumph of the Immaculate Heart. At Fatima on May 13, 1962, Cardinal Larraona Saralegui, papal legate for Pope St. John XXIII, said, "We must be assiduous in doing the Five First Saturdays of Reparation, not once but over and over again for those who will not or cannot do them." St. Maximilian Kolbe has also told us about this triumph, "The Immaculate Heart alone has from God the promise of victory over Satan. She seeks souls that will consecrate themselves entirely to her, that will become in her hand's forceful instruments for the defeat of Satan and the spread of God's kingdom."

DAILY CHALLENGE

Have you done the Five First Saturdays of Reparation yet? If not, make an effort to do them at least once. If you have done them once, do them again for someone else.

32. *"Speak ill of no one and avoid the company of those who talk (ill) about their neighbors."*

MEDITATION

Gossiping is one of the biggest sins of our time. It is no longer one person talking about another person. This sin has overtaken social media in all its forms. The horror of this sin was best illustrated by St. Philip Neri who assigned an unusual penance to a woman for her sin of spreading gossip. The 16th century saint had her take a feather pillow to the top of the church bell-tower, ripped it open, and scattered the feathers to the winds. The saint then added a more difficult task. He told her to come down from the bell-tower and collect all the feathers that had been dispersed throughout the town. Of course, this would be impossible to do. St. Philip Neri was making a point of the destructive nature of gossip. When we gossip, our malicious words are scattered abroad and can never be taken back. They continue to spread causing division to occur for days, months and even years after we have spoken them, passing from one person to the next. Pay heed to St. Paul's words on gossiping, "Do not let any unwholesome thought come out of your mouths, but only what is useful for building others up according to their needs that it may benefit those who listen." (Eph 4-29)

DAILY CHALLENGE

Today, when tempted to gossip, reflect often on the words of St. John Vianney, "If something uncharitable is said in your presence, either speak in favor of the absent, or withdraw, or if possible, stop the conversation."

33. "If men do not amend their lives, Almighty God will send the world, beginning with Spain, a punishment such as never has been seen."

MEDITATION

St. Jacinta spoke of "great world events" that were to take place around 1940. She was referring to the death and destruction of World War II, which claimed 40-50 million lives, the Jewish Holocaust, the widespread bombings of civilian populations and the atomic bombing of Hiroshima and Nagasaki. She cried when she thought of the catastrophe that was coming, because of the sins of men that were offending the Hearts of Jesus and Mary. Today, the world is once again on the precipice of a major world war, which will be more devastating than World War I and II combined. To prevent this, do as Our Lady asked at Fatima in 1917, pray your rosary every day, wear your brown scapular as a sign of consecration to her Immaculate Heart, offer up your daily duty and do the Five First Saturdays of Reparation.

DAILY CHALLENGE

What are you doing to bring about peace? Are you committed daily to fulfilling Our Lady's requests?

34. *"If governments left the Church in peace
and gave liberty to the Holy Religion,
they would be blessed by God."*

MEDITATION

St. Jacinta added to this insight when she said, "Pray a great deal for governments. Pity those governments which persecute the religion of our Lord. If the governments left the Church in peace and gave liberty to the Holy Religion, they would be blessed by God." Today Christians in Burma, China, Eritrea, India, Iran, Nigeria, North Korea, Pakistan, Russia, Saudi Arabia, Syria, and Vietnam are persecuted for their religious convictions. Among these, North Korea, consistently has one of the highest rates of persecution against Christians. St. Jacinta's words are more relevant today than ever before.

DAILY CHALLENGE

Today pray for governments that persecute the Church.

*35. When I'm alone, I get out of bed to recite the
Angel's prayer. But now I'm not able to touch the ground
any more with my head, because I fall over;
so I only pray on my knees."*

MEDITATION

During the first angel apparition in 1916, the angel taught the three children how to pray. The angel, with the three children, bowed low touching his head to the ground. After that apparition, the three children continued to pray with heads bowed low as the angel showed them. Prayer is the raising of one's mind and heart to God. We can pray anywhere, at any time. But the way in which, the angel taught the children to pray is a profound acknowledgment of our own nothingness and total dependence on God for everything.

DAILY CHALLENGE

Sometime today, when you are alone, if possible, pray as the angel at Fatima taught the three children to pray.

36. *"In church, we must be tranquil and not talk... Our Lady does not want people to talk in church!"*

MEDITATION

When I was a child you did not talk in church unless it was an emergency. Hushed whispers were rarely heard. Unfortunately, today this reverence for God in His church is ignored. People talk and carry on conversations, especially in front of the Blessed Sacrament. St. Padre Pio stated, "The language God enjoys most is silence." If you are excitable, anxious, obstinate, jealous or suspicious, especially when you enter a church, you will never have the peace needed to hear God's voice. God will not listen or speak to a noisy, dissipated and restless soul. When you enter a church, remember to leave the world outside, only then will you find the silence you need to hear God's words for you.

DAILY CHALLENGE

Today, think and reflect on the words of St. John Vianney, "How rare it is to find a soul quiet enough to hear God speak."

37. During a painful operation: *"Now you can convert many sinners for I suffer a great deal my Jesus."*

MEDITATION

We all have suffering in our lives. St. John Vianney said, "Our greatest cross is the fear of crosses." This applies to everyone. St. Jacinta instead of being fearful of her great pain and sufferings, accepted them as a way of savings souls. St. Padre Pio wrote on the great value of suffering: "Many suffer, but few know how to suffer well. Suffering is a gift from God; blessed is he who knows how to profit by it." How often do we waste the many opportunities to embrace our daily sufferings to save souls? We need to pray, especially to St. Jacinta, for help in overcoming our fear of suffering.

DAILY CHALLENGE

Suffering is the greatest treasure on earth for it purifies the soul. If today you are sent some form of suffering, little or big, look at the crucifix for courage!

38. *"You mustn't lie or be lazy or disobedient, and you must bear everything with patience for love of Our Lord if you want to go to Heaven."*

MEDITATION

Laziness is a sin against charity and leads one into temptations. It is the mother of all vices, and according to St. Paul, "For even when we were with you, this we commanded you, that if any would not work, neither should he eat. For we hear that there are some which walk among you disorderly, working not at all, but are busybodies. Now, them that are such, we command and exhort by our Lord Jesus Christ, that with quietness they work, and eat their own bread." (2 Thess. 3:10) St. Jerome tells us to "live in such a way that the devil will always find you busy." Concerning obedience, St. Francis de Sales wrote, "The devil doesn't fear austerity, but holy obedience, which without a doubt is more meritorious than any other penance." Finally, Our Lord said to St. Faustina, "Know that you give Me greater glory by a single act of obedience than by long prayers and mortifications."

DAILY CHALLENGE

Today, reflect on the words of St. Philip of Neri, "Obedience is a short cut to perfection." This is something we are called to, in order, to enter heaven.

39. *"Do you know why Jesus is so sad? Because Our Lady has explained how much He is offended and still nobody cares; they just go on committing the same sin."*

MEDITATION

Sin today is not only accepted but embraced. People sin without any regard for their immortal soul and many have become desensitized to sin. What would have shocked our parents and grandparents is considered acceptable today. Ven. Bishop Sheen wrote, "Sin is not the worst thing in the world. The worst thing in the world is the denial of sin." The philosopher Max Scheler said "while sin multiplies everywhere, the sense of guilt correspondingly diminishes." The Bishop of Fatima stated at Pontevedra on December 10, 1975: "In the light of the Fatima message, sin is not a phenomenon of the sociological order, but is, in the true theological concept, an offense against God with necessary social consequences. Perhaps no other century as the century we live in has had a life so sinful. But there is something new added in the sins of this century: the man of today, more sinful than those who came before him, has lost the sense of sin. He sins, but laughs and even boasts."

DAILY CHALLENGE

Pope St. Pius X said, "Do you know what is needed today? Rosaries – tens of thousands of rosaries." Today pick up your rosary and pray it for these obstinate, poor sinners.

40. On receiving communion: *"The Hidden Jesus! I love Him so much! If only I could receive Him in church! Don't they receive Holy Communion in Heaven? If they do, then I will go to Holy Communion every day. If only the Angel would go to the hospital to bring me Holy Communion again, how happy I would be!"*

MEDITATION

It is a fact that St. Jacinta received her first Holy Communion from the angel who appeared to them in the fall of 1916. She made her First Communion in 1918 and received Holy Communion several times during her short life. Unfortunately, she never received the Eucharist on her death bed. The little saint knew when she would die and asked to receive Our Lord. It was on the eve of her death, but the priest felt that she would not die that night and would return in the morning to give her Communion. Think of it, only several Holy Communions made her a saint. How many Communions have we made with little or no advancement in our spiritual life? St. Gertrude the Great said, "Every time a person receives Holy Communion, their place in heaven becomes greater and their stay in purgatory is shortened." St. Ignatius of Loyola added, "One of the most admirable effects of Holy Communion is to preserve the soul from sin." St. Jacinta's Holy Communions had this effect on her.

DAILY CHALLENGE

When was the last time you received Holy Communion? Remember it is the most important thing you can do and will shorten your stay in purgatory.

41. *"It's true! Today we haven't yet made a single sacrifice for sinners! We'll have to make this one."* Jacinta put the fig back in the basket and made the offering.

MEDITATION

St. Jacinta dearly loved eating figs, so this 'little sacrifice' was a 'great sacrifice' for the little saint. St. Therese of Lisieux gave us perspective on this type of sacrifice when she wrote, "Little sacrifices have a great impact and I prefer the monotony of obscure sacrifices to all ecstasies." Pope St. John Paul II said, "Jesus made suffering redemptive, either for our own soul or for the soul of another." Seventy-five years before the Fatima apparitions, St. John Vianney wrote, "It is beautiful to offer ourselves every morning in sacrifice to God and to accept everything in expiation of one's sins." This is exactly what Our Lady asked of everyone at Fatima to do – our daily duty.

DAILY CHALLENGE

Like St. Jacinta, what 'little sacrifices' that will come your way today can you offer up?

42. *"I love Our Lord and Our Lady so much, that I never get tired of telling them that I love them. I seem to have a fire in my heart, but it doesn't burn me."*

MEDITATION

Many saints have experienced this fire of divine love that St. Jacinta talks about in this quote. For example, St. Padre Pio, St. Catherine of Sienna, St. Francis of Assisi, St. Therese, St. Mary Magdalene de Pazzi and many others have experienced this 'burning love'. The experience of this fire of divine love does not even come close to God's total, unconditional love for us. Our Lord told Blessed Alexandrina Maria da Costa, "If you knew how much I love you; you would die of joy." Blessed Imelda was so consumed with the love of God that she died of love after receiving her First Holy Communion. That says it all!

DAILY CHALLENGE

When was the last time you spent time with Our Lord telling Him how much you love Him?

43. *"I don't say how but I saw the Holy Father in a very large house, kneeling before a table with his face in his hands. He was crying. Many people were in front of the house, some were throwing stones, while others were cursing him and using foul language. Poor Holy Father. We need to pray a lot for him."*

MEDITATION

St. Jacinta had a great love for the Holy Father, Christ's vicar on earth. This vision does not depict any particular pope, but it does represent the insults and irreverence, in general, for all the popes. The following popes, in particular, endured an onslaught of disrespect: Ven. Pope Pius XII during World War II, Pope St. Paul VI's concern and heartache over the disobedience of the hierarchy of the Church, and Pope St. John Paul II's attempted assassination, not to mention, the disobedience of some of the bishops along with the scandals within the Church. We need to pay heed to her impassioned words, "We need to pray a lot for him." Her love for him was so great that at the end of the rosary she prayed three *Hail Mary's* for his intentions.

DAILY CHALLENGE

When was the last time you prayed for Our Holy Father? In imitation of St. Jacinta, begin today to make an effort to pray every day for the pope, Christ's vicar on earth.

44. *"Oh, how much I love to suffer for love of Our Lord and Our Lady. They greatly love those who suffer for the conversion of sinners."*

MEDITATION

Love and the conversion of sinners is one of the themes of the Fatima message. St. Jacinta at a very young age understood this and lived it! This kind of suffering can mold and strengthen us to accept our crosses and sufferings to save sinners. Our Lord told St. Gertrude the Great, "The way of the cross is the royal road to heaven; suffering is the gate to our heavenly home." In the words of St. Ignatius Loyola, "If God sends you many sufferings; it is a sign that He has great plans for you and certainly wants to make you a saint." This kind of suffering with resignation and great love is a sign of predestination. When you are suffering, remember God has great plans for you and is calling you to be a saint!

DAILY CHALLENGE

Today, reflect on the words of St. Therese the Little Flower; "My God I *choose all*! I do not want to be a *saint by halves*. I'm not afraid to suffer for You. I fear only one thing: to keep my own will; so, take it, for I choose all that You will!" What small suffering can you endure, and offer up today, for the love of the two Hearts of Jesus and Mary?

45. "Luxurious living must be avoided;
people must do penance and repent of their sins.
Great penance is indispensable."

MEDITATION

When Our Lady told this to St. Jacinta, she entered into Our Lady's sorrow by saying, "I feel so sorry for Our Lady. I feel so sad." Once again, St. Jacinta's wisdom on overindulgence on the luxuries of the world is put into perspective today. The Church teaches luxury in itself is not sinful; it is what we do or do not do with our wealth and luxury that leads one to commit the sins of injustice and a failure in charity. In Sacred Scripture, Our Lord spoke about the wealthy man who wanted to know what was necessary to obtain eternal life. We know he left unhappy at Our Lord's words, "Go, sell all and follow Me!" Here is the root of the problem with an unhealthy attachment to our 'things'. When the wealthy young man was called to follow Jesus, he unfortunately chose his wealth. Blessed are the poor in spirit, for theirs is the Kingdom of God.

DAILY CHALLENGE

You need to ask yourself, what am I attached to, and like the wealthy man in the gospel, is it blocking your way to heaven?

46. Most offensive sin:

*"The sin which leads the greatest number of souls
to perdition are the sins of the flesh."*

MEDITATION

This, in my opinion, is one of St. Jacinta's most profound prophecies. One hundred years later this is the number one sin committed in the world today. Its enticements are everywhere you look: TV, internet, social media, cell phones and books. This evil is even infecting our children by their unprotected access to it through digital media and cell phones. Today, marriage is threatened to be obsolete, with the major assault on individual sexuality and sexual orientation. Hell is being flooded by these sins of these poor souls, who have no one to pray for them. Ven. Bishop Sheen said, "It used to be that we Catholics were the only ones who believed in the Immaculate Conception. Now everybody believes that he is immaculately conceived."

DAILY CHALLENGE

Prayer and penance are our only weapons against the impurity and immorality in the world today. Use these two weapons to save these poor, unfortunate souls!

47. *"If people only knew what eternity is, they would do everything to change their lives. People lose their souls because they do not think about the death of our Lord and do not do penance."*

MEDITATION

The problem with the world today is many people have embraced a very hedonistic lifestyle of 'eat, drink and be merry…' There is no thought about eternity, which is forever without end. Life is so fleeting and we have only one chance to live it right. God has given us this life to get to heaven. St. Julie Billart wrote, "Time is like loose change. It is given to us here below to buy the real things of eternity." St. Augustine adds to this thought in his writings, "Our one sole purpose in life is to gain merit for life in eternity." Whether we realize it or not, one day we all will be going from here to eternity.

DAILY CHALLENGE

It is important to resolve not to neglect meditating regularly on eternity and the value of your soul.

48. *"People are lost because they do not think of the death of Our Lord and do not do penance."*

MEDITATION

St. Jacinta's words reflect the very words of Our Lord in Luke 13:3: "No, I say to you: but unless you shall do penance, you shall all likewise perish." But why is it so important to meditate on the death of Our Lord, and why is this so important for our salvation? St. Bonaventure tells us, "He who desires to go on advancing from virtue to virtue, from grace to grace, should meditate continually on the Passion of Jesus." St. Peter of Alcantara gives us the reasons why this is so important for our salvation: 1) The bitterness of his sorrow, that we may be compassionate with him. 2) The greatness of our sins, which were the cause of his torments. 3) The greatness of this benefit, that we may be grateful for it. 4) That we may love him more fervently. 5) That we may be drawn to admiration of this great mystery of Our Lord's love for us. 6) That we may imitate and admire the virtues of our blessed Savior which shine forth in this great mystery.

DAILY CHALLENGE

The words of St. Bonaventure tell us why we should meditate on the passion and death of Our Lord: "He who desires to go on advancing from virtue to virtue, from grace to grace, should meditate continually on the passion of Jesus." These words should encourage you to make an effort every day to spend some time meditating on the passion and death of Our Lord.

49. *"Confession is a sacrament of mercy and we must confess with joy and trust. There can be no salvation without confession."*

MEDITATION

The Sacrament of Confession today is sadly neglected. The communion lines are long, but the confessionals are empty. St. John Bosco eloquently told us why confession is so important. "Do you want to become saints? Here is the secret: confession is the lock; confidence in your confessor is the key. This is how you open heaven's gates." The Sacrament of Confession is our way to heaven. St. Padre Pio described the beauty of a soul after confession, "If the poor world could see the beauty of the sinless soul, all sinners, all unbelievers, would be instantly converted."

DAILY CHALLENGE

When was the last time you went to confession? St. Vincent Ferrer told us the importance of confession when he wrote, "Confession is of such efficacy that it blots all sins from the Book of Death and the memory of the devil." Keep the devil guessing, and in the dark about your sins, and strive to go to confession at least once a month.

50. *"Priests must be very, very pure."*

MEDITATION

St. John Vianney tells us why a priest must be very pure when he said, "The priesthood is the love of the Heart of Jesus. When you see a priest, think of Our Lord Jesus Christ." A priest is another Christ – *Alter Christus*. The importance of the holiness and purity of a priest is explained by Ven. Fulton Sheen: "As the shepherd, so the sheep; as the priest, so the people. Priest-victim leadership begets a holy Church. Every worldly priest hinders the growth of the Church; every saintly priest promotes it. If only all priests realized how their holiness makes the Church holy, and how the Church begins to decline when the level of holiness among priests falls below that of the people!" Again, it is St. John Vianney who sums up why a priest must be very pure, "If I were to meet a priest and an angel, I should salute the priest before I saluted the angel. The latter is the friend of God; but the priest holds His place."

DAILY CHALLENGE

Today, and every day, say a prayer for pure and holy priests.

51. "Our Lady cannot at present avert the justice of her Son from the world. Penance is necessary. If people amend their lives, Our Lord will even yet save the world, but if not, punishment will come."

MEDITATION

"I shall be forced to let go the arm of my Son." These are the words of Our Lady of La Salette in 1846. Nineveh was saved because the people heard the words of Jonah: "Repent and do penance." Penance is any act or a set of actions done out of repentance for sins committed. Unfortunately, today, very few do penance for the sins of this world. God does not ask of us to do sack cloth and ashes. The penance required of everyone today is to accept and do their daily duty, which, in itself is a penance. St. Peter Damian wrote on penance, "The best penance is to have patience with the sorrows God permits. A very good penance is to dedicate oneself to fulfill the duties of everyday with exactitude and to study and work with all our strength."

DAILY CHALLENGE

We are all sinners and in need of doing penance, especially for the world. What small penance, that will come your way today will you accept and offer up for the sins of world and to console the hearts of Jesus and Mary?

52. *"You must pray much for sinners and for priests and religious. Priests should concern themselves only with the things of the Church".*

MEDITATION

On the priesthood, Ven. Fulton Sheen wrote: "The priest's time is not his own; it is Our Lord's." This is why St. Jacinta said, "Priests should concern themselves only with things of the Church." Ven. Sheen continued, "Who is going to save our Church? Not our bishops, not our priests and religious. It is up to you, the people. You have the minds, the eyes and the ears to save the Church. Your mission is to see that your priests act like priests, your bishops act like bishops, and your religious act like religious." Ven. Sheen finished, "The fall of the priest is completed by these steps: neglect of prayer, withdrawal to a distance from the Eucharistic Lord, dedication to a comfortable existence, negligence concerning occasions of sin and, finally, the substitution of a creature for Christ.

DAILY CHALLENGE

This same point was made over 1700 years ago by St. John Chrysostom: "Do you wish to know if the people of any place are righteous? Look at what sort of a pastor they have. If you find him pious, just, sound, believe the people will be the same, for they are seasoned with the salt of his wisdom. "The holiness of the people of God is dependent upon the sanctity of the priests. This is why we must pray for our priests and religious. Today pray for one priest.

53. "Disobedience of priests and religious to their superiors displeases Our Lord very much."

MEDITATION

Once again Ven. Fulton Sheen's wisdom explains to us what a priest should be. "Each priest is a man with a body of soft clay. To keep that treasure pure, he has to be stretched out on a cross of fire. Our fall can be greater than the fall of anyone else because of the height from which we tumble. Of all the bad men, bad religious men are the worst, because they were called to be closer to Christ." This explains why their disobedience displeases Our Lord so much. A disobedient priest can cause much damage to the Mystical Body of Christ. St. Alphonsus Liguori wrote about the power and responsibility of priests in regard to this: "With regard to the Mystical Body of Christ, that is, all the faithful, the priest has the power of the keys, or the power of delivering sinners from hell, of making them worthy of paradise, and of changing them from the slaves of Satan into the children of God."

DAILY CHALLENGE

Today there is a crisis in the Church concerning clergy. St. John Vianney said, "You must never speak against a priest." Hence, your job is not to criticize priests, but to pray for them. It is important to remember to pray for our priests.

54. *"Love poverty and silence."*

MEDITATION

Twice in Sacred Scriptures Jesus showed us His love of poverty: at His birth and at His death. Our Lord also told us the value of poverty in the Beatitudes: "Blessed are the poor in spirit for theirs is the kingdom of heaven." Yet, it was St. Francis of Assisi who called poverty, 'Lady Poverty', and said, "Grant me the treasure of sublime poverty." This goes hand-in-hand with silence. St. Teresa of Calcutta, also a lover of holy poverty wrote this on the value of silence: "We need to find God, and he cannot be found in noise and restlessness. God is the friend of silence. See how nature – trees, flowers, grass – grows in silence; see the stars, the moon and the sun, how they move in silence... We need silence to be able to touch souls." The call of Fatima is to save souls, and this is done through our silence which will enable us to hear God's gentle call.

DAILY CHALLENGE

Resolve to become a lover of silence. Try to make time today, to reflect in silence, the goodness of God in your life.

55. *"Have charity even for bad people."*

MEDITATION

We are all familiar with the quote from scripture, "Turn the other cheek." The saints all did this, but not as eloquently as St. Therese the Little Flower. There was a nun in her convent who was so difficult to deal with that the other nuns avoided her. St. Therese instead offered herself as this nun's servant. The other nuns witnessed the cruelty inflicted upon St. Therese by this elderly nun. Later the saint wrote on this particular nun and the problems she caused her; "What pleasure she has given me! I wish I could meet her now and give her a sweet smile."

DAILY CHALLENGE

Today, when you run into a difficult person, ask yourself, "How would I want to be treated and how would Jesus treat this person?"

56. *"Do not speak evil of people and fly from evil speakers."*

MEDITATION

St. Jacinta was justly concerned about speaking evil about people. Ironically, the people who speak ill of others and engage in gossip are hypocrites. They are nice when speaking face to face with people, but later, behind their backs, they will criticize, accuse and even verbally abuse the same person. They further hide their guilt and make light of their malicious comments. St. John Vianney said, "Indeed, my children, what could be more out of keeping with the holiness of our religion than impure language? It outrages God, it scandalizes our neighbor." The antidote for this type of hypocrisy is frequent confession.

DAILY CHALLENGE

Concerning these people who gossip and who will cross your path today, try to find the time to meditate on the words of St. Mother Teresa of Calcutta on what to do: "People are often unreasonable and self-centered. Forgive them anyway."

57. "Mortification and sacrifice please Our Lord very much."

MEDITATION

The saints have given us two excellent thoughts on mortification and sacrifice. St. John Vianney tells us, "Oh, how I like those little mortifications that are seen by nobody, such as rising a quarter of an hour sooner, rising for a little while in the night to pray when some people think of nothing but sleeping. We may refrain from warming ourselves. If we are sitting uncomfortably, we need not try to place ourselves better; if we are walking in our garden, we may deprive ourselves of some fruit that we should like; in preparing the food, we need not eat the little bits that offer themselves. We may deprive ourselves of seeing something pretty, which attracts our eyes, especially in the streets of great towns." It is Jesus who told St. Faustina what He wanted: "My daughter, you give Me most glory by patiently submitting to My will, and you win for yourself greater merit than that which any fast or mortification could ever gain for you...I take great pleasure in it; there is power in it. Know that when you mortify your own self-will, then Mine reigns within you."

DAILY CHALLENGE

Today will you sacrifice your own will and accept all that God will send you this day to please Him and help save souls?

58. *"To be a religious one must be very pure in body and mind."*

MEDITATION

Those in the religious life take vows of poverty, chastity and obedience freely and publicly. The vow of purity allows one to have a deeper and closer relationship with God. It also helps to avoid all occasions of sin because one's focus is on attaining perfection and union with God. St. Teresa of Calcutta, in one simple statement, has told us how to achieve this purity of body and mind: *"Purity is the fruit of prayer."* Therefore, for anyone to achieve purity they must be faithful in their daily prayer life whether in the religious life or in the world, for we are all called to be pure in body and mind.

DAILY CHALLENGE

Purity in the world today is a difficult challenge. We must remember that in the gospels, Our Lord said, "Blessed are the pure of heart for they shall see God." Use this quote as your reflection and meditation, continuing to pray every day for purity.

59. *"Woe to the women wanting in modesty! ...Women are worse than men on account of the fashions."*

MEDITATION

This prophetic statement of St. Jacinta should make us careful on how we dress. When we dress immodestly, we become an occasion of sin to everyone we meet. It is the prophecy attributed to St. Nilus (5th Century) which gives us much to meditate upon: "After the year 1900, toward the middle of the 20th century, the people of that time will become unrecognizable...People's appearances will change, and it will be impossible to distinguish men from women due to their shamelessness in dress and style of hair." But it is the words of St. Jerome on modesty that cry out through the centuries to the sinful and immodest generation of today. "Either we must speak as we dress, or dress as we speak. Why do we profess one thing and display another? The tongue talks of chastity, but the whole body reveals impurity."

DAILY CHALLENGE

Resolve not to become a slave to the fashion industry thereby becoming an occasion of sin to everyone you meet.

60. *"God does not wish the death of the sinner.*
He wants them to convert, to give glory to God
on earth and in heaven."

MEDITATION

How does one convert a sinner? I am sure we have all asked ourselves this question, especially when it concerns our loved ones who have left the Church. We accomplish this by the Morning Offering of our daily duty. In the gospels we read of Veronica's small service of wiping the face of Jesus, which was heroic because it was done for Christ. In the morning, when we offer our thoughts, words and actions of this day to God, we turn them into "little Veronica's Veils" not only for the suffering Body of Christ, but also for poor hardened sinners who have no one to pray for them. This is the power we have to convert sinners.

DAILY CHALLENGE

When life throws you curve balls today, turn them into 'little Veronica's Veils,' to offer up patiently and so like St. Paul you can say, "I fill up what is lacking in the sufferings of Christ." (Col 1:24) This is how you will convert sinners. What will you offer up and do today for the conversion of sinners?

61. St. Jacinta picked up her favorite prayer from Fr. Cruz: *"Sweet Heart of Mary be my salvation."*

MEDITATION

Sr. Lucia wrote: "Jacinta chose, from the litany of suggested ejaculations, this one: *'Sweet Heart of Mary, be my salvation!'* She sometimes added 'I so love the Immaculate Heart of Mary! It is the Heart of our dear Mother in heaven! Don't you love saying many times over, *Sweet Heart of Mary, Immaculate Heart of Mary?* I love it so much, so very much.' Other times, as she gathered wildflowers, she sang a tune that she made up: *'Sweet Heart of Mary, be my salvation! Immaculate Heart of Mary, convert sinners, save souls from hell!'"* This short prayer has a partial indulgence when recited with devotion and was taken from the following:

> *Sweet Heart of Mary,*
> *make my heart love like thine for Jesus burn.*
> *O Heart aflame with heavenly fire,*
> *to learn this love, to thee I turn.*
>
> *Light in my heart this conflagration.*
> *Sweet Heart of Mary be my salvation.*
> *Sweet Heart of Mary, purest heart,*
> *no whitest lily can compare,*
>
> *With spotless purity like thine,*
> *O Mary, take me to thy care.*
> *In every danger and temptation,*
> *Sweet Heart of Mary be my salvation.*

DAILY CHALLENGE

Pray often *'Sweet Heart of Mary, be my salvation!'*

62. *"I would give anything to be able to go up to the Cabeco and say a rosary there in our favorite place, but I am not able to anymore."*

MEDITATION

In this quote, St. Jacinta here is teaching us the value of prayer especially praying the rosary. But she has taken it a step further by her desire to pray in the places where she prayed the rosary: In her favorite place where the message began when she saw the angel of peace. It was while she was very ill and confined to her bed that she expressed this desire to Lucia. How important is your prayer life to you? How often do you pray, especially in church in front of the tabernacle where Jesus is truly present? Do you make this effort to pray at least a 5-decade rosary every day?

DAILY CHALLENGE

Today, in imitation of St. Jacinta try to make an effort to pray, especially the rosary.

63. As St. Francisco was dying, Jacinta said to her brother: *"Give all my love to Our Lord and Our Lady and tell them that I'll suffer as much as they want for the conversion of sinners and in reparation to the Immaculate Heart of Mary."*

MEDITATION

We all need to realize that Christianity did not do away with dying. Just as Christ had to die, in order to enter into His glory, so too all of us must die. It is not dying that makes one a saint but how well one lived. Christ's passion, death and resurrection gave a new meaning to death. We all must accept the death God will send us. One beautiful prayer to pray every day is, "Eternal Father I accept with a joyful and resigned heart the death you will send me with all its pains and sufferings." It is credited to St. Alphonsus Liguori that, "cheerfully embracing that kind of death which God is pleased to send, and at the time and in the manner in which God sends it, one can render themselves like the holy martyrs." The saint further emphasized in his writings on preparation for death, "that offering one's death to God, particularly by cheerfully accepting the death God sends, constitutes a most perfect act of divine love." He suggests that this act can make one like the holy martyrs.

DAILY CHALLENGE

Remember it is not morbid to reflect upon death, but wise common sense to do so, for it is only after our death that we will really begin to live.

64. Lucia explaining St. Jacinta's high degree of understanding on prayer and penance and willingness to suffer: *"In my opinion it was a special grace granted to her through the Immaculate Heart of Mary and through the vision of hell and the unfortunate souls fall into it."*

MEDITATION

Not all of us will receive the graces that St. Jacinta received, but we all receive the graces we need to become saints. The doorway to sanctity has a double lock. Doing our daily duty, simply and without fuss, is the outside key. This daily duty includes praying, doing penance and being willing to suffer all that God will send your way on any given day. When we pray, work, and sleep all to please God, and for the love of God, that is the inside key. It is the inside key that is the greatness of a soul. St. Jacinta understood this and embraced it every day of her short life.

DAILY CHALLENGE

Every day you have two choices; one to reject and complain about your daily duty, the other is to accept all that God will send you today by saying, "For you Lord." Which one will you choose today?

65. *"Oh, Hell! Hell! How sorry I am for the souls who go to hell! And the people down there, burning alive, like wood in the fire!"*

MEDITATION

Lucia wrote that Jacinta often sat thoughtfully on the ground or on a rock, exclaiming these words. She then shuddered; kneeling down with her hands joined and recited the prayer taught to them by Our Lady: *"O my Jesus, forgive us our sins, save us from the fires of hell. Lead all souls to heaven, especially those in most need of your mercy."* This prayer is known as the Decade Prayer and is prayed after each decade of the rosary at the request of Our Lady.

DAILY CHALLENGE

Recite the Decade Prayer often today, offering it for poor souls who have no one to pray for them.

66. On making sacrifices;
"Jesus, this is for your love and for the conversion of sinners."

MEDITATION

We all want to make sacrifices for the love of Jesus, but as it is written in scripture, "The spirit is willing, but the flesh is weak." Like the Apostles in the Garden of Gethsemane, we are all weak. It is through the offering of our daily duty that we can overcome our weak human nature. Upon waking every day, pray your Morning Offering. It is this prayer that will call us to moments of quiet prayer with Jesus throughout our day. It does not matter how long this time of quiet prayer lasts; whether it is a few moments or even an hour in church before the Eucharist, it is this quiet prayer that will console the Heart of Jesus and bring about the conversion of sinners.

DAILY CHALLENGE

It is up to you today to make those little moments of quiet time of prayer with Jesus happen.

67. *"Doctors do not know how to cure people properly, because they have not the love of God."*

MEDITATION

This particular quote of St. Jacinta has more meaning today than it did in 1920. With the advent of modern medicine, and the great strides made in curing diseases, doctors need to acknowledge that it is God who works through them to heal the sick. He has given them the necessary skills to treat their patients. Yet, the many medical professionals today do not realize that they must work with God when taking care of the sick. It is their love of God and acknowledgment of His gifts, and knowledge of healing that enables them to take care of their patients. A good doctor needs to pray every day to God for himself and for the patients entrusted in his care.

DAILY CHALLENGE

Remember to pray today for all who work and take care of the sick.

68. From time to time she would cry out to her brother, *"Francisco! Francisco! Are you praying with me? We must pray very much to save souls from hell! So many go there! So many!"*

MEDITATION

Though she was very young, St. Jacinta understood the seriousness of the reality of hell. She took to heart the request of Our Lady to pray and offer sacrifices for sinners. It can be said that the vision of hell was a turning point in her spiritual life. Blessed Anna Maria Taigi was shown how many souls went to hell on one day, she said, "They were as numerous as snowflakes in mid-winter." Many of the saints have said the same thing about the great number of souls that are lost.

DAILY CHALLENGE

Today, remember to pray for those who are dying this day. Pray that Our Lord's mercy will be their salvation.

69. When Jacinta saw Lucia in tears, trying to console her she said, *"Don't cry. Surely, these are the sacrifices which the angel said that God was going to send us. That's why you are suffering, so that you can make reparation to Him and convert sinners."*

MEDITATION

What a beautiful and consoling sight this must have been. St. Jacinta finds her cousin crying; reaching out with compassion and love, she reminds Lucia that this sacrifice came from God so she could make reparation and convert sinners. How many of us console someone with just a hug and a quick, 'It will be ok' or 'I will say a prayer for you.' What a missed opportunity to remind each other that every moment in our day is a grace that can be accepted to offer up and save sinners. St. Jacinta is an example for all of us to imitate.

DAILY CHALLENGE

Every day is an opportunity to console and help those we love. What a wonderful opportunity for you to gently remind them that their sufferings are not in vain but to help to save sinners.

70. *"Why doesn't Our Lady show hell to sinners?*
If they saw it, they would not sin, so as to avoid going
there. You must tell Our Lady to show hell to all the people.
You will see how they will be converted."

MEDITATION

After the vision of hell, St. Jacinta was consumed with saving souls from that *'awful place.'* She was convinced that if everyone saw hell, they would not go there. At the time of Jacinta's death, the vision of hell was one of the three secrets that had not yet been released. In the scriptures, Our Lord refused to tell the Dive's brothers on earth about the existence of hell. Taken from Lk. 16:19-31 on the parable of Dives and Lazarus. He said they had the prophets and scripture and that was sufficient. The vision of hell was given for our age when Christians would down play the idea of eternal punishment or even deny its existence. According to a 2021 Pew Research Center survey, 1 in 4 Americans do not believe in hell. That is a large number of souls in danger of going to hell. This vision was a great grace obtained by Our Lady for our sinful generation.

DAILY CHALLENGE

Hell is a reality that people today refuse to believe. Today, pray one *Hail Mary* for a poor dying soul that does not believe in hell that they may be saved.

71. *"Tell them that they should all ask for peace*
from the Immaculate Heart of Mary,
as God has placed it in her hands."

MEDITATION

In order to understand why St. Jacinta made this statement, Ven. Sr. Lucia would later write what Our Lord Himself explained to her about His desire to establish this devotion. Our Lord said, "I desire most ardently the propagation of the cult of the devotion to the Immaculate Heart of Mary, because the love of this Heart attracts souls to Me; it is the center from which the rays of My light and My love go through all the earth, and the unquenchable fountain from which the living water of My mercy flows into the earth." As St. John Eudes wrote, "The hearts of Jesus and Mary are truly one heart." This is why St. Jacinta said that we must ask for peace from the Immaculate Heart of Mary because God has placed this peace in her hands.

DAILY CHALLENGE

Pray this day – and every day – for peace and ask for it from the Immaculate Heart of Mary.

72. *"Be very charitable, even with those who are unkind. Never criticize others and avoid those who do."*

MEDITATION

We have been told since we were young to avoid bad companions and occasions of sin. We all know people in our lives who are unkind and critical of everyone they meet. We are not expected to spend time with these kinds of people, but we must pray for them. Christian charity requires us to do this. It is through persistent prayer that people change and amend their lives. Do not be the harbinger of evil and gossip. St. Paul in his letter to the Ephesian (4:29) wrote: "Let no corrupt communication proceed out of your mouth, but that which is good to the use of edifying, that it may minister grace unto the hearers."

DAILY CHALLENGE

Today when you are tempted to gossip or criticize others, reflect on the following quote: "When we judge or criticize another person, it says nothing about that person; it merely says something about our own need to be critical."

> 73. *"Be very patient, for patience brings us to heaven.*
> *Mortifications and sacrifices please our Lord a*
> *great deal."*

MEDITATION

The patience of Jesus throughout His entire life, especially during His passion and death, is an example for everyone showing us that in patience we will possess our soul. Our Lord further showed us that silence is the language of patience. Yet the great St. Francis de Sales gave us the best advice on patience: "Have patience with all things, but chiefly have patience with yourself. Do not lose courage in considering your own imperfections, but instead set about remedying them – every day begin the task anew." It is this virtue of patience that will bring us to heaven.

DAILY CHALLENGE

Do you give way to annoyances, exasperations, anger; criticizing others when they fall short of your expectations? It is during these times and other times of impatience that we need to remind ourselves the need of praying for patience, especially with yourself.

74. *"The Mother of God wants a large number of virgin souls to bind themselves to her by the vow of chastity. I would enter a convent with great joy, but my joy is greater because I am going to heaven."*

MEDITATION

St. Teresa of Calcutta wrote, "We take vows of chastity to love Christ with undivided love." She was referring to the beautiful virgin souls that dedicate their lives to Christ and His Church when they enter a convent/monastery. This refers to either a cloistered or active religious community. Today there is a serious decline of generous souls responding to God's call to the religious life. This relates to the secularism in the world today. People are only concerned about themselves and not the giving of themselves that is required with a religious vocation. The call is given, but so few respond with a generous heart.

DAILY CHALLENGE

Pray today for generous souls to respond to God's call to the priesthood and religious life.

75. "Do you know what it means to be pure?"
Mother Godinho asked the young saint.
"Yes, I do. To be pure in body means to preserve chastity.
To be pure in soul means to avoid sin, not to look at what
is sinful, not to steal, never lie and always tell the truth
even when it is hard. Whoever does not fulfil promises
made to our Lady will not be blessed in life."

MEDITATION

"Blessed are the pure of heart for they shall see God." The will to be pure is necessary, but it is not enough. We need grace to be pure and we must pray for this grace every day and avoid all unnecessary occasions of sin. St. Francis de Sales tell us, "Be exceedingly quick in turning yourself from every form and allurement of lewdness. This evil works insensibly, and from small beginnings it advances to great troubles. These are always easier to avoid than to cure." Our best protection against temptations of impurity is stay out of its radar, with a mind and body well-occupied with doing God's will. The beauty of purity is best described by St. John Bosco, "Holy Purity, the queen of virtues, the angelic virtue, is a jewel so precious that those who possess it become like the angels of God in heaven, even though clothed in mortal flesh."

DAILY CHALLENGE

Our challenge today comes from St. Alphonsus de Liguori, "We must practice modesty, not only in our looks, but also in our whole deportment, and particularly in our dress, our walk, our conversation, and all similar actions."

76. *"I am suffering a lot. But I offer everything for sinners and in reparation to the Immaculate Heart of Mary."*

MEDITATION

Once again we see the theme of suffering in the life of St. Jacinta. The world today shuns and runs away from all forms of suffering, whether it is physical, mental, spiritual, financial or within our families. Yet, what have the saints written and said about suffering? St. Teresa of Avila tells us, "Suffering can serve as an active form of prayer, if we allow it." While St. Gemma Galgani further tells us, "When I shrink from suffering, Jesus reproves me and tells me that He did not refuse to suffer." This is something we all need to meditate and reflect upon; the fact that Our Lord did not refuse to suffer for us. We need to remember that suffering is a great grace, and it is only through suffering that we become like Jesus. The greater the suffering, the purer the love of the sufferer.

DAILY CHALLENGE

Pope St. John Paul II said, "Don't waste your suffering." This is coming from a pope who spent most of his life suffering, especially for the Church. Today, try not to waste your sufferings; rather, embrace them and save souls.

77. *"The more I think the more I suffer, and I want to suffer for love of Our Lord and for sinners."*

MEDITATION

When we are suffering, we all cry out in pain and pray like Our Lord, "Father, let this chalice pass from me." Just as Christ trembled at the thought of His passion and death in the garden of Gethsemane, so too, for us to tremble at pain is Christlike. We need to realize that suffering is not a good thing that merely appears evil, but it is an evil that our humanity shrinks from, by nature. But the grace of God can sanctify our suffering. Grace sanctified the suffering of the saints, especially the suffering of St. Jacinta.

DAILY CHALLENGE

Today, if pain and suffering come your way, pray for the grace to accept and sanctify it so that you may save not only your soul, but also for poor souls who have no one to pray for them.

78. At times, Jacinta kissed and embraced a crucifix exclaiming, *"O Jesus! I love You, and I want to suffer very much for love of You."*

MEDITATION

Ven. Patrick Peyton, the Family Rosary Priest, wrote, "The gate of heaven has a cross for a key. My cross can be another's key. To unite my sufferings to Christ's for the salvation of souls is the highest form of apostolic zeal." This is what St. Jacinta did when she united her sufferings with that of Jesus's sufferings. She truly possessed the virtue of zeal. True zeal, which inflamed her pure heart, is active, insatiable and gentle and prudent. Finally, never become discouraged and never despair the salvation of anyone. Like St. Jacinta, you must use all the means in your power to convert sinners especially the most hardened ones.

DAILY CHALLENGE

Today, try to maintain a good disposition and a peaceful heart so that everyone you meet will be open to God's grace of conversion.

79. *"Our Lord must be pleased with our sacrifices, because I am so thirsty, so thirsty! Yet, I do not want to take a drink. I want to suffer for love of Him."*

MEDITATION

Jesus said from the cross, "I thirst!" There was the extreme physical thirst that Our Lord suffered, yet His cry while on the cross, "I thirst!" was more a spiritual thirst for souls. As in the Garden of Gethsemane, His thirst was for the many souls that would of their own free will choose hell for all eternity instead of their salvation merited by the passion and death of Our Lord. We need to realize that the reason for our existence is to quench this thirst of Jesus just as St. Jacinta did when she said, "I am so thirsty."

DAILY CHALLENGE

Today, what small sacrifice can you accept, and do with great love to quench the thirst of Our Lord for souls?

80. When people asked her questions, she answered in a friendly manner, but briefly. If they said anything which she thought improper, she promptly replied: *"Don't say that; it offends the Lord Our God."*

MEDITATION

Before the apparitions, St. Jacinta was a very talkative child. After the first apparition on May 13, she was told by Lucia not to tell anyone what they saw. But all she could say was, "Oh, what a beautiful lady!" When she went home, she promptly told her parents about the 'beautiful lady'. This was the beginning of Lucia's difficulties and sufferings, especially with her mother. When Jacinta realized she was the cause of her cousin's suffering, she apologized. From then on, she was very quiet and did not talk much. If questioned, she answered it briefly and politely. Ven. Fulton Sheen gives a great explanation on the value of silence: "In silence, one awakens from his sleep; all souls are sleepwalkers, their eyes shut against the noble lives they ought to lead. As a sleepwalker will not awaken to every sound but will often respond when his name is called, so the soul in silence hears the Divine vocation and awakens; for the Shepherd calls His sheep by name." We all need to remember that Jesus shamed Pilate by His silence!

DAILY CHALLENGE

Do you think before talking and answering questions? Do you always want your opinion heard? Today, stop, think and pray before voicing your opinion. Remember the old adage, "Silence is Golden."

81. If people related something unbecoming about their families, St. Jacinta answered: *"Don't let your children commit sin, or they could go to Hell."*

MEDITATION

Parents have the serious responsibility to raise their children Catholic and to make sure they receive the sacraments. The Church teaches that the family is the domestic church where we live and teach our faith. *The Catechism of the Catholic Church* (#1656) tells us, "In our own time, in a world often alien and even hostile to faith, believing families are of primary importance as centers of living, radiant faith. For this reason, the Second Vatican Council, using an ancient expression, calls the family the *Ecclesia domestica.*" Again, the CCC #2685 relates, "Based on the holy Sacrament of Matrimony, the family is the 'domestic church' where God's children learn to pray 'as the Church' and to persevere in prayer." We do this by praying together, especially the family rosary, attending Mass together every Sunday, reading Scripture daily and spending time in adoration in church. Parents are answerable to God on how they raised their children. Children are gifts from God, on loan to parents whose job is to make sure they give back to God this most precious treasure.

DAILY CHALLENGE

For parents, raising saintly children in this sinful and immoral world today is a difficult challenge. Today, pray for all parents that they will take this responsibility seriously by invoking the aid of Holy Family, the role model for all families today.

82. One day Lucia asked St. Jacinta: *"What are you going to do in heaven?"* She answered, *"I'm going to love Jesus very much, and the Immaculate Heart of Mary, too. I'm going to pray a lot for you, for sinners, for the Holy Father, for my parents and my brothers and sisters, and for all the people who have asked me to pray for them..."*

MEDITATION

Have you ever thought about 'what you are going to do in heaven?' Is your response as generous and loving as St. Jacinta's was to her cousin Lucia? Consider the promise of St. Therese the Little Flower; "Upon my death I will let fall a shower of roses; I wish to spend my heaven in doing good upon the earth." The Church teaches us that there is the Church Militant on earth, the Church Suffering in purgatory and the Church Triumphant in heaven. The saints in heaven love to help us here on earth on our journey to eternity. Turn to them often for help in all your needs and necessities.

DAILY CHALLENGE

Who is your go-to saint when you need help? If you do not have a particular saint that you pray to, start reading about the saints and find the one that 'speaks' to your heart.

WORKS CITED

Coelho, Sr. Angela de Fatima, *Inside the Light, Understanding the Message of Fatima,* Tan Books, Gastonia, NC 2020

Fox, Robert J. Father. *Fatima Today,* Christendom Educational Corporation 1983.

Libreria Editrice Vaticana. *Catechism of the Catholic Church.* New York: Pauline – St. Paul Books and Media, 1994.

Madigan, Leo, *The Children of Fatima,* Our Sunday Visitor Publishing Division, Huntington, IN 2003

Medeiros, Humberto Sousa, *Jacinta, The Flower of Fatima,* Tan Books, Charlotte, NC 2017

Rengers, Christopher. *The Youngest Prophet.* New York: Alba House, 1986.

Sr. Lucia of Jesus and of the Immaculate Heart. *Fatima in Lucia's Own Words.* Massachusetts: The Ravengate Press, 2000.

The New American Bible. New York: Thomas Nelson Publishers, 1986.

ABOUT THE AUTHOR

Catherine Moran, OFM, is a speaker, author and radio personality. She is the president of the World Apostolate of Fatima (Blue Army) Byzantine Division in Ohio, and a member of the National Board of Trustees.

She is the author of *Mary's Gentle Path, Daily Meditations from the Writings of Sister Lucia*, a companion to this book. As custodian of the Pilgrim Virgin Icon of Our Lady of Fatima, she appeared on EWTN LIVE with Fr. Mitch Pacwa, to discuss the importance of the Fatima message for the Eastern and Western Catholic Churches. She helped coordinate the WAF USA 2016-17 Fatima Centennial US Tour for Peace with the world-famous International Pilgrim Virgin Statue and has chaired the statue's visitation to her eparchy.

Moran has hosted several shows on Radio Maria, including Homeschool Lifeline, Am I Not Here, Go to Joseph and her most recent, Beyond Fatima. She also co-hosts the podcast "Fatima Today".

She was part of the delegation of Catholic homeschool leaders that met with Pope St. John Paul II in 1995 and 1997 and Pope Benedict XVI in 2006 to discuss Catholic homeschooling in the United States. The delegation was privileged to receive Holy Communion from Pope St. John Paul II.

Moran is a Third Order Franciscan and a member of Holy Trinity Ukrainian Byzantine Catholic Church. She and her beloved husband, Dave, have five children – two adopted from Ukraine – and eight grandchildren. They reside in Niles, Ohio.